Animal Habitats

The Rabbit in the Fields

Text by Jennifer Coldrey

Photographs by
Oxford Scientific Films

Gareth Stevens Publishing
Milwaukee

This country scene shows several different kinds of fields in which rabbits are living.

Where rabbits live

Rabbits are found in many different countries around the world. They can survive almost anywhere, providing it is not too hot or too cold and there is plenty of grass or other green food to eat. The most common are the wild European rabbits, which came originally from northwest Africa, Spain, and Portugal. From here they spread through central Europe and were first brought to Britain by the Normans in the 12th century. Later, human beings introduced them to other parts of the world, including Australia, New Zealand, Asia, South America, and western parts of North America.

The hedgerow along the edge of this field is an ideal place for rabbits to hide.

A rabbit on the alert at the edge of a field.

Rabbits often live in and around the edges of fields. They like to feed in grassy meadows, and especially in *pastureland* where the grass is kept short by grazing cattle or sheep. They are found in *cultivated* fields, too, and may do a lot of damage by eating crops that the farmers grow.

Rabbits need to find shelter as well as food. They live above ground or in burrows underground, but when they come out to feed, they need other places to hide, too. They prefer to live in small fields surrounded by hedges, dry stone walls, or a border of trees and shrubs, into which they can quickly dash for cover if danger threatens. They are not so common in the large open fields of modern *arable* farms. Here there is nowhere to hide, and the farmers are continually plowing and disturbing the land with their big, heavy machines.

Rabbits are shy and timid creatures with many enemies to fear. They come out of their burrows mainly at night to feed and explore, and it is not always easy to see them during the day. The best time to look for them out in the fields is at dusk or dawn. You may also be lucky enough to see them in the daytime in quiet, undisturbed places.

Rabbits leave plenty of signs in the countryside which show they are about. Look out for scrapes in the ground and holes leading down into a burrow. Check tracks and footprints in mud or snow and look for droppings. Other clues include runs or pathways through the grass and bits of rabbit fur caught on hedges or barbed wire.

Here are the tell-tale signs of rabbits — some fur caught on a bramble, and a tunnel through the grass.

The warren

Rabbits are social animals and live together in family groups. The underground home of many rabbits is a complicated network of tunnels and burrows called a warren. The female rabbits do most of the hard work of building the warren. The tunnels they dig are about 6 inches (15cm) wide, large enough for a rabbit to move through easily. A warren usually has several different entrances and exits, including some very small *bolt-holes*, only 2½ inches (6cm) or so across. These are just big enough for a rabbit to escape through in an emergency, but too small for many *predators* to follow. Some tunnels in a warren are very short. Others may go down as deep as 10 feet (3m) underground, with side branches into nest-burrows and other tunnels. Rabbits find it easier to dig their burrows in light, sandy, well-drained soils. They often choose sloping ground, which helps prevent water settling and flooding their burrows after heavy rain.

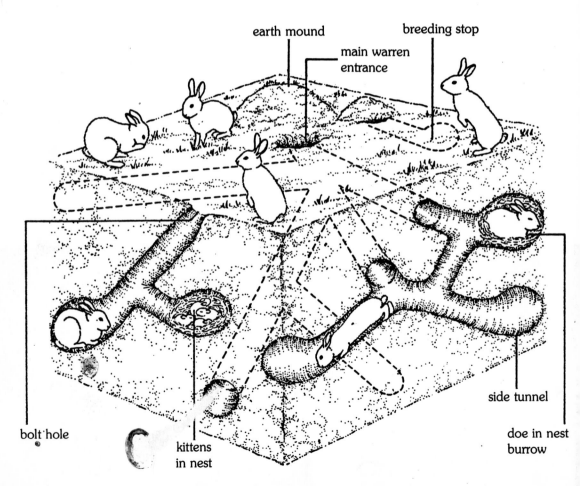

earth mound

breeding stop

main warren entrance

side tunnel

bolt hole

kittens in nest

doe in nest burrow

A young rabbit peeps out from one of the holes into its burrow.

These rabbits spend a lot of time in the shelter of their underground homes. Here they are protected from the cold and from their enemies. The burrow is a safe, warm place for rabbits to sleep and rest, to digest their food, and to give birth and rear their babies.

Warrens become bigger as rabbits breed and continue to enlarge their system of underground tunnels. Smaller warrens cover only a few acres of ground, but larger ones can be enormous, and may spread over several fields.

You should be able to spot a rabbit warren quite easily. The main entrance hole is usually marked outside by mounds of soil which the rabbits have dug out from below ground. Other clues will be tracks and droppings, and the grass will be closely nibbled and trodden down around the various entrances.

The underground tunnels are just big enough for a rabbit to pass along easily.

The rabbit's body

Rabbits are soft, furry animals. The wild European rabbit has a thick, soft coat of greyish-brown fur. It has a rusty-red patch on the back of the neck, and white underparts. The short white tail is held upturned, close to the body, and is dark on the upper side. The coloring can vary quite a lot, and wild rabbits are sometimes found with black, white, or sandy-colored coats. Rabbits *molt* their fur once a year, starting in the spring. The molting starts on the face and gradually spreads back and down over the rest of the rabbit's body. By the autumn they have a much thicker coat which keeps them warm during the winter.

A fully-grown European rabbit measures about 16 inches (40cm) long and weighs up to 4 pounds (2kg). There is very little difference between males and females, although the male (called a *buck*) has a broader head and is usually slightly bigger than the female (called a *doe*).

In North America, Cottontail rabbits are much more common than European rabbits. They look very similar and behave in much the same sort of way, but there is one important difference. Cottontails do not make burrows underground. Instead they sleep and nest above ground, in holes or hollows in the grass, or under bushes and rocks.

A male and female European rabbit – the doe is on the right.

This Cottontail rabbit lives in central and eastern parts of North America.

Rabbits have big round eyes and long, pointed ears. Their eyes are set on the sides of their head, giving them a good all-round view of their surroundings. Rabbits can see quite well in the dusk as well as in daylight. But their sense of hearing is even better than their eyesight, and they can pick up the faintest sounds by twisting and turning their long, sensitive ears in various directions.

Rabbits have an excellent sense of smell. Their nostrils are constantly sniffing and twitching to pick up scents in the air. When a rabbit opens its nostrils it pulls back a covering of skin and exposes two special pads which are very sensitive to scents. The long, dark whiskers sticking out from the sides of the nose are sensitive to touch.

Even in dim light, rabbits can see quite well with their big round eyes.

A close-up of the rabbit's muzzle shows its nostrils and the long, curved incisor teeth.

This photo of a rabbit's skull shows the jaw bones clearly, and the large gap between the front and back teeth.

Rabbits have two kinds of teeth. At the front are the *incisors* (two pairs on the upper jaw, one pair on the lower jaw). These are sharp, strong teeth with chisel-shaped ends, useful for cutting and biting. Further back are the cheek teeth or *molars*. They have flat, ridged surfaces, and are used for grinding and chewing food. There is a large gap between the front and back teeth, and this can be useful. When a rabbit gnaws on wood or other hard things with its incisors, it closes off the back of its mouth by pinching in the skin on each side of this gap. This prevents any dirt or rough chippings being swallowed. A rabbit's teeth never stop growing, but they are prevented from becoming too long and dangerous because the rabbit wears them down by continually gnawing on trees and other woody plants.

When a rabbit digs, it cuts into the soil with its front paws and kicks out the dirt behind with its back legs.

The rabbit's white tail bobs up and down as it hops along.

Legs and movement

The front legs of a rabbit are small and neat. Each foot has five toes with claws, and these are useful for digging. Rabbits dig to find food and also to make their homes. The back legs are longer and more powerful than the front legs. They have strong muscles which are especially useful for pushing the rabbit forwards when it jumps or leaps. Rabbits do not walk or run. They jump or hop along the ground, lifting their back legs up high and landing on their front paws.

When frightened, they bound along extremely quickly, reaching speeds of up to 15 miles (24km) per hour. At high speeds their back legs come down on the ground in front of their front legs. You can see this when you find their tracks in mud or snow. The soles of a rabbit's feet are covered with hair. This helps it to grip on rocks or slippery slopes, as well as on snow and ice. Rabbits can stand up and balance quite well on their long back paws, each of which has only four toes with claws.

These rabbit tracks in the snow show the larger back feet landing in front of the front feet, which means that the rabbit was moving quickly.

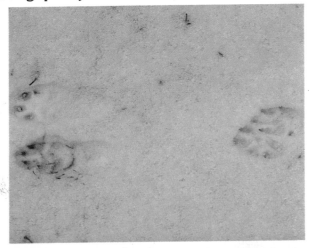

In quiet, undisturbed fields, rabbits will come out in the day-time to feed on the grass.

Food and feeding

Rabbits are vegetarians — they eat only plants — and they have very large appetites. Like all plant-eating animals, they need to eat large amounts of food in order to get enough energy to survive. A rabbit can eat at least 1 pound (500g) of fresh green food a day. Rabbits eat a lot of grass, as well as many other leafy plants that grow in the fields, such as clover, daisies, prim-roses, and sorrel. They also enjoy eating many cultivated plants, especially the young green shoots of wheat and barley, as well as kale, cabbage, peas, and lettuce. They dig up roots to nibble, such as carrots and turnips. In fact, it is no wonder rabbits are disliked by many farmers and gardeners!

Rabbits are choosy eaters. They prefer short grass and tender young shoots and will not touch tough, coarse grasses or plants like ragwort, thistles, and nettles. In pastureland they nibble only the best grasses and eventually spoil the grazing for sheep and cattle.

This young rabbit nibbles away at some juicy cow-parsley plants.

In wintertime, fresh green food is hard to find.

Rabbits are out and about all the year round. In winter food is more difficult to find, especially if snow and frost cover the ground. Rabbits then nibble the bark from trees, especially young *saplings*, and this often causes serious damage. When young trees are planted around the edges of fields, or in other places where rabbits live, people put special guards made of plastic or wire netting around the trunks to protect them.

The trunk of this hawthorn tree has been badly damaged by rabbits gnawing at the bark.

Digestion

Rabbits do most of their feeding at night, when they are safer from their enemies. On bright, moonlit nights they stay close to their homes, ready to dash to safety should danger threaten. When they have eaten their fill, they return to their homes and start to digest their food. Plants are difficult to digest and do not provide enough nourishment when they pass through the rabbit's *intestine* just once. The rabbit therefore eats its first droppings, which again pass through the intestine before the final droppings are produced.

Rabbits come out, mainly at night, to look for food. This one nibbles at a fern on the edge of the woods.

Back in its burrow, this rabbit eats its first droppings, which are soft, moist pellets of half-digested food.

While resting in its home during the day, a rabbit produces soft, moist, round pellets of half-digested food. These are the first droppings which it immediately swallows. They pass into its stomach again and the food is digested for a second time. Later, when the rabbit comes out in the evening, it produces a different kind of dropping. These are the final droppings — dry pellets of waste food, which are dropped above ground. These dry droppings are often left in special places near the home, forming a rabbit's *latrine*. You can sometimes find piles of droppings on top of an anthill or on an old tree stump.

A pile of dry rabbit droppings, like this, is a good clue that rabbits live nearby.

Rabbits spend a lot of their time cleaning and grooming their fur.

Behavior

Rabbits are very clean animals. They never foul their homes with urine and droppings, and they spend a lot of time cleaning and grooming themselves. They wash their fur by licking it, and they also comb through their fur with the claws on their feet. To wash their faces, they lick their forepaws and cover the pads with saliva, which they then rub over their ears and head.

Rabbits can sometimes be seen during the day in quiet, undisturbed places, especially if the weather is fine and warm. They like to stretch out and doze in the sunshine. They will also feed and explore if they are left in peace. They do not like cold, wet, or windy weather and will spend most of the time in their shelter if the weather is bad.

Rabbits never wander too far away from the safety of their homes, even at night. They rarely go further than about 200 yards (180m) away. They are home-loving creatures and are closely attached to the area around their homes and to the company of other rabbits.

There are some rabbits, usually bucks, which live alone and never join a warren. They don't live in burrows, but make their homes in scrapes or hollows under stones, shrubs or bramble bushes. These bucks are usually the weaker, more timid animals which have been forced out of the warren where they were born and have not been able to find a doe, or to fight for a place in another warren.

This handsome buck is stretching out to enjoy the sunshine on a warm summer day.

A family group outside their warren.

Social life

Many rabbits — especially European rabbits — live in large groups or colonies. Some colonies are small, with no more than 10 or 12 animals, but others can be enormous, with several hundred rabbits living together. However, within a large warren, there are usually smaller family groups, with up to 24 members.

There is a definite social order within each family group, the older and stronger rabbits holding more important positions than the younger or weaker ones. There are usually more does than bucks, with the most senior buck as head of the family. His job is to look after the does and young and to defend the group against attack from enemies, including other male rabbits.

A buck rabbit marks out his *territory* and shows that it belongs to him by leaving his scent. He does this by squirting urine and leaving droppings in various places. Rabbits also have a special *gland* under the chin which produces a strong-smelling liquid. This they rub onto plants or against the ground to leave their scent.

A buck rabbit stands on guard, alert and ready to defend his family against intruders.

Bucks do so much of this "*chinning*" that they often rub the fur quite bare under their chins. Does have chin glands too, but they do not scent-mark nearly as much as bucks do.

During the breeding season buck rabbits can be very aggressive to each other. They show their anger with special threat displays, such as scraping the ground with their front paws; grazing with short, sharp bites as they move towards their rival; or by hopping around their opponent in an awkward stiff-legged movement.

A weaker buck usually recognizes a stronger buck and either runs away or lies down flat, with ears laid back, in a position of defeat. However, male rabbits often come to blows when they are fighting for does or for the chance to claim a territory of their own. The fights are often fierce and vicious and sometimes end in death. When fighting, rabbits bite and kick each other, pulling out fur with their claws and often wounding each other. Does rarely fight, although they can be aggressive when they are looking after their young.

Here a buck marks out his territory by rubbing the scent from his chin onto a plant.

The buck and doe chase each other around in an excited courtship dance.

Mating and breeding

Rabbits can breed at any time of year, although the main breeding season lasts for five to six months from winter through to early summer. A buck usually mates with several does. He starts his courtship by dancing around a doe in small circles. If she is interested, she will join him in the dance, flicking up her tail as they leap and chase one another around. When the doe is ready to mate, she crouches on the ground and lifts up her hindquarters. The buck mounts her from behind and mates. Then he usually topples over sideways onto the ground beside her. A buck and doe may stay together quietly, side by side, for some time after mating, affectionately licking and nuzzling each other.

After mating, the pregnant doe starts to make a nest for her babies. In warrens, older, more senior does make their nests within the main warren in special, short, unbranched burrows. Younger does build a separate nest burrow, 3-6 feet (1-2m) long, just outside the main warren. This is called a *breeding stop*. The doe collects grass, moss, and leaves to line her nest. She also pulls fur from her belly to make a soft, warm bed for her babies. Bucks play no part in making the nests or rearing the young.

When she is ready to mate, the doe lets the buck climb onto her back.

This pregnant doe is collecting grass with which to line her nest.

The baby rabbits (or kittens as they are called) are born four weeks after mating. They have no fur and cannot see or hear. Each kitten weighs only 1½-1¾ ounces (40-50g). There may be as many as ten kittens in a litter, although there are usually between three and six, and occasionally only one or two. The kittens feed on their mother's milk. She visits her babies once each night to suckle them. When she leaves the stop she covers the entrance with earth to disguise the hole and keep out predators. Her action also helps to keep the kittens warm.

These one-day-old rabbit kittens are blind and deaf and have no fur.

At six days, this baby rabbit now has fur and its teeth and claws have started to show.

Growing up

Baby rabbits grow quickly. After four days their fur is showing through and they are able to hear. By the end of the first week their weight has doubled and their teeth and claws are visible. Their eyes open around the tenth day, and by the time they are three weeks old they have already started to explore the world outside their burrow. Here they nibble the grass and start to learn about the many dangers around them, while the doe stays nearby to guard them.

By four weeks, the young rabbits are fully *weaned* and the mother leaves them to fend for themselves. The doe is usually pregnant again by this time, and she starts to make another nest for her next litter. Female rabbits usually mate within a day or two of giving birth. They can have as many a seven litters in one season, which could mean 30-40 young in a single year. In fact, this happens rarely, because many of the embryos die at an early stage in pregnancy and are reabsorbed into the mother's body. This is common when there is overcrowding in a warren or a shortage of food. It prevents too many babies from being born in times of hardship. Most does only have about 10 or 12 young a year. Young rabbits reach adult size at nine months old. They are able to breed before they are a year old, the does at only three or four months.

By 12 days old, the kittens' eyes are open.

Now 18 days old, this young rabbit is ready to explore the world outside its burrow.

This means that a young doe born early in the year can have her own babies by the end of the summer. No wonder we speak of "breeding like rabbits"!

Towards the end of the breeding season a group often becomes overcrowded and many of the younger rabbits are driven off in search of other homes. Young bucks are more adventurous than does. They sometimes wander far and wide during their first year, some living alone, while others are lucky enough to join another group or to find an empty burrow to live in. Most young bucks eventually want to start a colony of their own. They often have to fight for does and for a home of their own.

These two young bunnies, at four weeks old, will now have to fend for themselves.

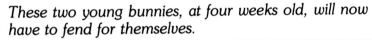

This fox, out hunting at night, has caught a rabbit and is dragging it back into the woods.

Predators and other dangers

Rabbits have a lot of enemies. They are killed and eaten by many animals including foxes, badgers, stoats, weasels, rats, dogs, and both wild and domestic cats. In some parts of the world they are attacked by wolves, coyotes, dingoes, skunks, and snakes. Foxes and badgers often dig out baby rabbits from the breeding stops, while rats, weasels, and stoats can chase rabbits down into their burrows underground, even through the narrowest tunnels.

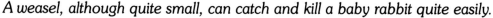

A weasel, although quite small, can catch and kill a baby rabbit quite easily.

A hawk swoops down to catch a rabbit out in the open.

Birds of prey, including eagles, hawks, buzzards, and owls, swoop down on them from the air, while crows, magpies, and ravens feed on dead or injured rabbits.

Young rabbits are especially at risk from all these enemies. They are not as strong as adults and have not yet learned to react so quickly to signs of danger. More than three-quarters of all young rabbits die before they are three months old, and very few survive their first year. Many are killed by predators, while others die from disease or from cold and starvation during their first winter. On flat areas of land, flooding of the burrows after heavy rain can also cause the death of baby rabbits in their nests. Those in deeper burrows are the most likely to drown. People are also enemies of the wild rabbit, as we shall see later.

Defense

Rabbits are weak and timid creatures. They cannot easily defend themselves against attack. Instead they rely on their quick, alert senses to help them escape from danger before it is too late. If a rabbit senses danger it will sit up on its hind legs, erect and still, with its ears pricked and nose twitching. This behavior will put other rabbits on their guard, too. Rabbits have many ways of signalling DANGER to each other. When they hop away quickly their white tails bob up and down, making an obvious sign of alarm to other rabbits. Another warning signal is to thump on the ground with their back legs. This is especially useful at night when rabbits cannot see each other clearly.

Rabbits are usually silent, but if they are trapped or injured they let out a high-pitched scream. This is almost certainly a cry of pain, but it may also act as a warning to other rabbits to run for safety.

When danger is near, rabbits lie low in the grass with their ears laid back.

A rabbit watches out, with all its senses on the alert for signs of danger.

Rabbits usually stay quite close to their burrows or to some sort of cover, so that they can dash for shelter when danger threatens. Their dull greyish-brown covering helps to *camouflage* them against their surroundings, and they are often difficult to see in the dim light of dusk and dawn. When they are very frightened, rabbits crouch low on the ground with their ears laid back. They stay absolutely still so that predators will not notice them.

One of the best ways of escape is to disappear down the nearest burrow.

These dead rabbits have been shot. People shoot rabbits for sport, as well as to keep their numbers down.

Rabbits and humans

Throughout history human beings have had a great effect on the lives of rabbits. It was mainly because of humans that rabbits spread or were introduced to many different parts of the world. In Britain in the middle ages, for example, rabbits were kept in special enclosures where they were bred for meat and fur. Noblemen also hunted them for sport. They later escaped into the surrounding countryside, where they spread and increased rapidly in numbers. Farming methods changed during the 18th and 19th centuries — fields were enclosed by hedgerows and crops were grown throughout the winter. This was marvelous for rabbits! They bred even faster and became a terrible pest to farmers all over the country in the 19th and early 20th centuries. People tried to control them by various methods of shooting, trapping, snaring, and gassing, but this was never very successful, and one or two rabbits always managed to escape to carry on breeding.

This man is putting a ferret down a rabbit's burrow to chase out the rabbits into nets, which are placed over the other exit holes.

Then, in the early 1950's, a deadly disease called myxomatosis came into Britain from Europe. It quickly spread through the rabbit population and killed millions of animals. This disease, which came originally from South America, was also deliberately taken to France, Australia, and New Zealand, to try to control the enormous numbers of rabbits which were destroying so much of the plant life there. As in Britain, practically all the rabbits were killed.

Myxomatosis is a *virus* disease. It is carried from one rabbit to another by blood-sucking insects like mosquitoes or fleas. The disease causes nasty, jelly-like swellings on the head and hind-quarters of the rabbit. The eyelids swell up and stick together and the rabbit becomes blind and deaf. It gradually dies a slow and horrible death which can take from 11 to 18 days.

Fortunately a few lucky rabbits survived or escaped the disease. They continued to breed and gradually became more resistant to the virus. Although myxomatosis still kills some rabbits every year, it is much less deadly than it was, and rabbits are once again quite common in the countryside. They can still be a pest to farmers and landowners and have to be killed whenever their numbers become too great. Rabbits are hunted for sport even today, and people also kill them for food and to use their fur for clothing.

A rabbit suffering from myxomatosis. The small picture shows a rabbit flea (about 1mm long) which carries the disease from one rabbit to another.

Hares are bigger than rabbits, with long ears and extremely long back legs.

Friends and neighbors in the fields

Many other animals live alongside rabbits in fields and meadows. Mice and voles, shrews, frogs and toads, snakes, and many insects share the same *habitat*. Birds like partridges, plovers, and skylarks often nest among the clumps of grass, while other birds like starlings, crows, and pigeons, come to feed on grain or on insects in the soil.

Hares, which are closely related cousins of the rabbit, also live in the fields. Hares are much bigger than rabbits, with longer, black-tipped ears and large back legs. They eat the same food and live the same sort of life as rabbits do, but they cause less damage in the fields because they eat much less and do not breed as rapidly as rabbits. Unlike many rabbits, all hares live alone and above ground. They seldom mix with rabbits, but seem to live quite happily in the same surroundings.

This hedgehog has made its nest in a deserted rabbit burrow.

Moles tunnel underground and sometimes come into contact with rabbits. Other animals, such as foxes, rats, hedgehogs, and badgers sometimes make their homes in deserted rabbit burrows. Rats even use the rabbits' nesting material for their own nests. Rabbits, in their turn, sometimes use the empty burrows of other animals for their homes — American Cottontails often live in the deserted burrows of badgers, prairie dogs, skunks, or woodchucks.

In pastureland rabbits share the grazing with cattle and sheep, horses, and even pigs. If woods are nearby, deer may come down into the fields at night to graze on the grass and crops.

Rabbits like to live in fields where the grass is kept short by grazing sheep.

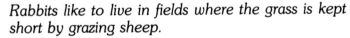

Life in the fields

Rabbits are an important food supply for many animals that come to hunt for prey in and around the fields. Rabbits depend on plants for their food. The plants they eat are used to build up their bodies and to give them energy to live. Rabbits in their turn are eaten by various meat-eating animals, so a lot of this food and energy is then passed on to them. In this way a food chain is built up. We can see this more clearly by drawing a diagram to show some of the food chains involving rabbits.

Food chain

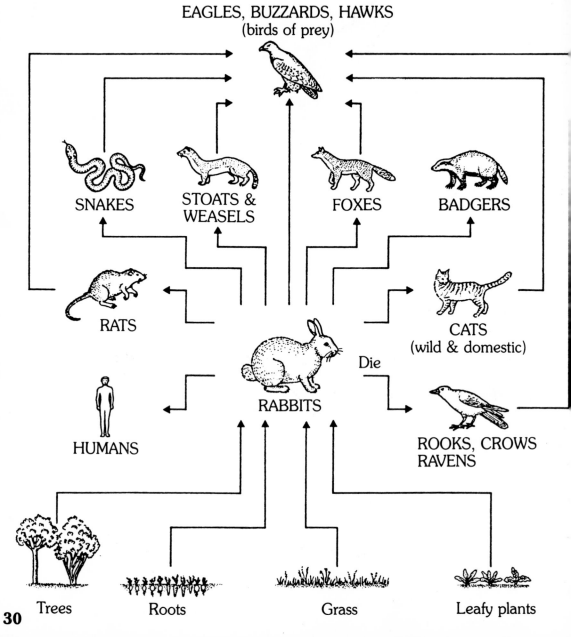

EAGLES, BUZZARDS, HAWKS
(birds of prey)

SNAKES

STOATS &
WEASELS

FOXES

BADGERS

RATS

CATS
(wild & domestic)

HUMANS

RABBITS

Die

ROOKS, CROWS
RAVENS

Trees

Roots

Grass

Leafy plants

Rabbits living round the edges of this field have caused a lot of damage to the growing crops.

Rabbits still survive in many fields, in spite of the threat from modern farming.

Rabbits are a nuisance to farmers in the fields. Besides eating food crops, they spoil the good quality of the grass in meadows and pastures. Their burrowing disturbs the ground and allows weeds to grow. Farmers, in their turn, cause considerable harm to rabbits and their habitat and it is modern farming methods that are largely to blame. In order to create large, open fields for their huge crops of cereals, farmers have once again cleared away many trees and hedgerows, so that there is hardly anywhere for rabbits to live. Large heavy farm machines continually disturb the ground, killing many rabbits and destroying their underground burrows. In addition, the crops are sprayed with weedkillers, *insecticides*, and other chemicals which often poison the land and harm many of the animals living in the fields.

However, in spite of the constant threat from human beings and from their many other enemies, rabbits somehow always manage to survive. They are quick-witted and alert, escaping quickly from danger to safety. But the main reason they are so successful is because they breed so rapidly. Although few wild rabbits live to be much older than two years, one pair of rabbits can produce millions of descendants in only three years!

Life in the fields is not always easy for them, but, providing there are some quiet and sheltered places left in the countryside, rabbits are unlikely to die out completely.

Glossary

These new words about rabbits appear in the text in italics, just as they appear here.

arable . . . . suitable for plowing and growing crops
bolt-holes . . . . small holes through which to escape
breeding stop. . . . . short nesting burrow outside a main warren
buck . . . . male rabbit
camouflage . . . . . . animal disguise; how an animal hides by looking like its surroundings
chinning . . . . rubbing the chin against plants or the ground to leave a scent
cultivated . . . . land which is used for growing crops
doe . . . . female rabbit
gland . . . . part of the body which produces a special substance such as sweat, milk, or digestive juices
habitat . . . . the natural home of any animal or plant
incisors . . . . long, sharp, cutting teeth at the front of the rabbit's mouth
insecticides . . . . . . poisonous chemicals which people spray on crops to protect them from insect damage
intestine . . . . part of the digestive system below the stomach
latrine . . . . lavatory
molars . . . . back teeth of rabbits (and all other mammals) which are used for crushing and grinding food
molt . . . . to shed hair or fur and replace it with a new coat
pasture(land) . . . . grassland used for grazing sheep or cattle
predators . . . . animals that kill and eat other animals
saplings . . . . young trees
territory . . . . piece of land which an animal defends against intruders
virus . . . . microscopic organism which causes disease inside animals or plants
weaned . . . . (of young animals); no longer dependent on their mother's milk for food, but now able to eat other things

Reading level analysis: SPACHE 3.4, FRY 5, FLESCH 7.7 (fairly easy), RAYGOR 6, FOG 7, SMOG 5.7.

Library of Congress Cataloging-in-Publication Data

Coldrey, Jennifer.
   The rabbit in the fields.

(Animal habitats)
Summary: Text and illustrations depict rabbits feeding, breeding, and defending themselves in their natural habitats.
   1. Rabbits — Juvenile literature. [1. Rabbits] I. Oxford Scientific Films. II. Title. III. Series.
QL737.L32C649   1986   599.32'2   85-30298
ISBN 1-55532-086-4
ISBN 1-55532-061-9 (lib. bdg.)

North American edition first published in 1986 by Gareth Stevens, Inc., 7221 West Green Tree Road, Milwaukee, WI 53223, USA.

Text copyright © 1986 by Oxford Scientific Films. Photographs copyright © 1986 by Oxford Scientific Films.

Conceived, designed, and produced by Belitha Press Ltd., London. Typeset by Ries Graphics ltd. Printed in Hong Kong. U.S. Editors: MaryLee Knowlton and Mark J. Sachner. Design: Treld Bicknell. Line Drawings: Lorna Turpin. Scientific Consultants: Gwynne Vevers and David Saintsing.

The publishers wish to thank the following for permission to reproduce copyright material: **Oxford Scientific Films Ltd.** for pages 2 *below right*, 6, 7 *below left*, 8 *above and below*, 9 *above and below*, 10 *below*, 11 *above and below*, 12, 13 *above and below*, 14, 15, 16 *below*, 17, 18 *above and below*, 19 *above and below*, 20 *above and below*, 21 *above and below*, 22 *above*, 24, 25 *above and below*, 26 *above and below*, 29 *above*, and 31 *left and right* (photographer G. I. Bernard), page 1 (photographer P. K. Sharpe), page 2 *above* (photographer Raymond Blythe), page 2 *below left* (photographer David Cayless), page 7 *above* (photographer M. P. L. Fogden), pages 10 *above* and 27 (photographer David Thompson), page 16 *above* (photographer Chrissie Houghton), page 22 *below* (photographer Avril Ramage), page 29 *below* (photographer Sally Foy); British Natural History Pictures for pages 3, and 7 *below right* (photographer John Robinson); Aquila Photographics for page 23 (photographer Dennis Green); Survival Anglia for page 28 (photographer Dieter Plage). Front cover photographer: G. I. Bernard. Back cover photographer: David Cayless.